Weight Loss & Wellness
Guided Meditation

Labyrinth

Welcome to the exciting world of Creative Meditation

The guidebook is designed to work in correspondence between you and your God Source.

Meditation is one way to connect to this Source for the purpose of co-creating and manifesting magnificence in your life.

Regular practice of this guided meditation will help raise your energy level up to a vibration that God Source and the law of attraction can and will respond too.

Shifting your energy and raising your vibration upwards opens a channel for you to communicate with your higher power and this is the first step towards manifesting your magnificence.

Creative Meditation is a combination of guided imagery, color visualization, gentle movement and positive re-enforcement, designed to put you in the receptive mode for manifesting magnificence.

Meditation is an ancient art, yet a simple technique that anyone can practice and learn.

Regular meditative practice is an excellent tool for releasing and reinvigorating your energy field so that you are in receptive mode for manifesting.

Through meditation you will learn how to generate pure positive energy, raise your vibrational frequency, and how to keep up the momentum daily. The law of attraction responds to your vibrational attitude and will bring you more and more of what it is you are feeling and thinking about.

Your ability to manifest is not a question. Everything in your life up to now you have created. Maybe by default in some cases, but you can change that.

The question is what kind of energy are you projecting and thereby attracting back into your life? This meditation is designed to help you align your energy and raise your vibrational atmosphere to a place where you are able to receive whatever it is you desire; the ideal body, job or relationship.

To Begin:

First it is important to get your frame of mind in a place of peace. Once you get into a comfortable position, meditation begins with a focus on your breathing. Slowly and deliberately you inhale, pause and exhale as you witness your breathing.

Thoughts will come in and your job is to not get attached to the thought, just let it go. Bring yourself to focus on your breathing each time you drift off into thinking. Once you have been practicing meditation for a while thoughts interfere less often.

So don't despair. There is no right or wrong way to meditate. It is not necessary to remain completely still during meditation. Move your shoulders and arms and shift your body anytime. Invite your guardian angel or your spirit guide into your meditation if you choose.

Progressive Muscle Relaxation is the first step in this meditation. PMR technique is simple. Begin with a focus on your feet. Contract your toes, hold that position for 5 seconds and relax. Do this several times from your toes, up your legs, torso, hands, arms, neck, shoulders, face and head.

By now your body is now completely relaxed.

The Nasal Snore: As you inhale slowly bring your breath up toward the back of your nasal openings, pause a second, then slowly exhale as if you are doing a slight snore, this creates the relaxation response quickly.

Feel the relaxation sensations travel throughout your body, permeating every cell and every atom of your being. Allow yourself to drift down into a state of sheer relaxation. Allow the relaxation sensations to permeate every cell and every atom of your Being. Allow this feeling to sink in.

Anytime during the meditation you can use the nasal snore. There is no right or wrong way to meditate. Thoughts will come, but for now see them as floating clouds and let them go on by. Just breathe.

Now imagine in your mind's eye and stand witness to the color energies surround you & travel along your spine column, into your vertebrae, along nerve pathways, into your internal organs and nervous systems, nourishing your cells, your organs and tissues.

Color vibrations intermingle with the electromagnetic emanations of your body and internal systems. They communicate through a very sophisticated language know as bio-photons. Your own internal organs and systems resonate and respond to the these energies.

In your mind's eye imagine the latticework or grid work being filled in with bluish green ocean energies. See the colors help to rearrange and straighten out any trapped energy that might be submitting a dark or murky color in your grid. These dark colors are actually stuck energies and need to be awakened and reactivated.

Now we will calm the part of your aura called the mental body. On an EEG machine your mental body extends 5 – 6 inches out from the physical body and is like a lattice or grid with a blue grey swirling cloud pattern that is uniquely yours.

This is important work in order for you to move forward on this issue you carry in your energy field.

Let these color energies fill your grid, clearing away anything that does not match your desired energy for an ideal body weight. Breath in the pure positive energy that is you. As you relax into this feeling of wonderment, think of yourself as energy, see yourself as energy, just for now don't think of yourself as a dense physical body, just think of yourself as energy.

Can you feel yourself as energy? Can you feel yourself as this energy moves through and around you? Doesn't it feel wonderful? Isn't it exhilarating?

You are doing a very powerful exercise and with regular practice you will manifest with effortlessness.

Now think of your aspiration to lose weight [be successful, financial freedom] as a wreath of energies that you have been carrying around for a long time now.

Bring your awareness to any murky energy that might be lurking in your vibration. Bring soothing light green energy into any murky areas.

In your mind's eye witness the area transform into a healthy well-lite grid. See the color energy as it begins to permeate the dark and add sparkles until the murky stuck energy is all lite up. See the clearing away of anything that does not match your desire.

The Law of Attraction responds to your vibrational frequency. What you are emitting and what you are sending out will return to you.

The universe operates and communicates via electromagnetic waves and you have your very own unique magnetism.

he universe is continually listening to your vibration and responding in kind. Like attracts like.

Allow these color energies to fill your grid, clearing away anything that does not match your desired energy for an ideal body weight.

As you relax into this feeling of wonderment, think of yourself as energy.

Can you feel yourself as energy? Can you feel yourself as this energy moves through and around you? Doesn't it feel wonderful? Isn't it exhilarating?

You are doing a very powerful exercise and with regular practice over the next 30 days you will build and manifest with effortlessness and peace.

You have added new vibrations to your own energy. For you are one with that which Creates. All that matches you must come to you. This is the law of the universe; The Law of Attraction

If it is something you have wanted to create for a long time, your energy match is already close, all you have to do is make the necessary vibrational adjustment

This is all about raising your vibration to match the vibration where everything you want already is.

Today you have begun.

Before we begin our ascent back into physical reality, now is a good time to repeat the following affirmations:

AFFIRMATIONS

No longer is my focus on self-control or will-power, this is not about self-control, not about will-power. This is about changing my vibrational frequency.
As long as I got my eye on where I want to be I am distracted from where I don't want to be. This is important work for me to realize.

Lamenting about where I am now at will only slow down the process of who I am becoming and my job is to make peace with the here and now

By deactivating negative conversations about what it is I don't have yet and by focusing on the feelings of pure positive deliberate potential of becoming, each day I see a gradual improvements

I can be happy now where I am. My most important work right now is to raise my vibration to a point where I feel joy as I grow and move forward on my life's journey. When I am too busy realizing who I have been in the past, I am slowing down who I am becoming. I am becoming. I am becoming. I don't have to figure it all out today, but I do want to be a cooperative component with the laws of creation.

 I so love learning new ways of looking at life.
I realize now that I am a magnet of pure positive energy and I came forth with great reason and purpose.
I came here to experience life, not as an observer, but as an active participant, a co-creator. No matter how I am viewed here in my physical body. My physical body is only a fraction of who I really am.

I am excited to see what I can attract in my life during this 30 day practice and I know once I get the momentum going in the right direction, nothing can stop me.

The universe delivers to me that which I feel.

I have a better understanding now of where I am going in relation to my physical body.

Day by day I shift my vibration and raise myself up to where I belong.

Each day I receive a clearer vision of my purpose.

Each day I see a gradual improvement. I resolve to make peace with who I am and what I look like because I know this physical reality is only a very small fraction of who I really am.

I resolve to stop punishing myself for not being who I have been reaching for.

I am in a state of becoming

I am making a deliberate effort to shift my energy away from negativity.

Each day I see a gradual improvement
And I have energies that create worlds standing at my back.

Remember, these ripples of energy are invisible only to the naked eye. Science and technology reveal to us just how very real this energy field is. These are the energies that create worlds. These energies are an extension of you and they continue to permeate throughout your physicality hours after your meditation is over.

You have just performed a very important exercise and should give yourself and your guardian angels thanks. Practice for 30 days. Come back tomorrow.

Revel in this ecstasy and if this is your bed time, now is a great time to fall asleep.
If it is not nap time, then begin to move your hands and arms and legs to reinsert yourself back into the material world.
Care enough about yourself to practice.
Believe in yourself and your abilities. There are forces far greater than yourself that are assisting you. You are learning to be a cooperative component.
The powers that be would like to see you successful as well.

Never waver or doubt yourself. Carry yourself like a diamond in the sky. A shift will occur on the cellular level and stay with you as you go about your daily life.

Dear Reader
I do hope this book has in some way helped you in your quest for health and wellbeing.
Please contact me with any feedback and comments, I'd love to hear from you @ jenally55@gmail.com

CPSIA information can be obtained
at www.ICGtesting.com
Printed in the USA
BVHW05s1605020418
512247BV00033B/1106/P